JUV   Color and light.
QC
495.5
.C64
1993

$18.60

DATE			

HANDS-ON SCIENCE

COLOR AND LIGHT

Step-by-Step Science Activity Projects
from the Smithsonian Institution

Gareth Stevens Publishing
MILWAUKEE

For a free color catalog describing Gareth Stevens' list of high-quality books, call 1-800-542-2595 (USA) or 1-800-461-9120 (Canada). Gareth Stevens' Fax: (414) 225-0377.

Library of Congress Cataloging-in-Publication Data

Hands-on science: color and light / by Megan Stine . . . [et al.] ; illustrated
    by Simms Taback.
        p. cm. — (Hands-on science, step-by-step science activity projects from the
    Smithsonian Institution)
    Series originally published by the Smithsonian Institution as a series of science
activity calendars.
    Includes bibliographical references and index.
    Summary: Suggests a variety of experiments, recipes, and other activities
demonstrating the properties of color and light.
    ISBN 0-8368-0954-8
    1. Color--Experiments--Juvenile literature.   2. Light--Experiments--Juvenile
literature. [1. Color--Experiments. 2. Light--Experiments. 3. Experiments.
4. Scientific recreations.] I. Stine, Megan. II. Taback, Simms, ill. III. Series:
Hands-on science (Milwaukee, Wis.).
QC495.5.H36   1993
535'.078--dc20   92-56889

Produced and published by
Gareth Stevens Publishing
1555 North RiverCenter Drive, Suite 201
Milwaukee, Wisconsin 53212, USA

Series editor: Patricia Lantier-Sampon
Book Designer: Sabine Beaupré
Editorial assistants: Jamie Daniel and Diane Laska

Printed in the United States of America

2 3 4 5 6 7 8 9 99 98 97 96 95 94

CONTENTS

Weights and Measures Abbreviation Key

U.S. Units

in = inch	oz = ounce
ft = foot	qt = quart
tsp = teaspoon	gal = gallon
T = tablespoon	lb = pound
C = cup	°F = °Fahrenheit

Metric Units

cm = centimeter	kg = kilogram
m = meter	km = kilometer
ml = milliliter	°C = °Centigrade
l = liter	
g = gram	

INTRODUCTION

By the 21st century, our society will demand that all its citizens possess basic competencies in the fundamentals of science and technology. As science becomes the dominant subject of the workplace, it is important to equip children with an understanding and appreciation of science early in their lives.

Learning can, and does, occur in many places and many situations. Learning occurs in school, at home, and on the trip between home and school. This book provides suggestions for interactive science activities that can be done in a variety of settings, using inexpensive and readily available materials. The experiments, activities, crafts, and games included in this book allow you, whether teacher or parent, to learn science along with the children.

SOME SUGGESTIONS FOR TEACHERS

The activities in this book should be used as supplements to your normal classroom science curricula. Since they were originally developed for use in out-of-school situations, they may require some minor modifications to permit a larger number of children to participate. Nonetheless, you will find that these activities lend themselves to a fun-filled science lesson for all participants.

SOME SUGGESTIONS FOR PARENTS

One of the most important jobs you have as a parent is the education of your children. Every day is filled with opportunities for you to actively participate in your child's learning. Through the **Hands-On Science** projects, you can explore the natural world together and make connections between classroom lessons and real-life situations.

FOR BOTH TEACHERS AND PARENTS

The best things you can bring to each activity are your experience, your interest, and, most importantly, your enthusiasm. These materials were designed to be both educational and enjoyable. They offer opportunities for discovery, creative thinking, and fun.

HOW TO USE THIS BOOK

There are ten activities in this book. Since every classroom and family is different, not all activities will be equally suitable. Browse through the book and find the ones that seem to make sense for your class or family. There is no prescribed order to these activities, nor any necessity to do all of them.

At the beginning of each activity is a list of all the materials you will need to do the project. Try to assemble all of these items before you begin. The procedures have been laid out in an easy-to-follow, step-by-step guide. If you follow these directions, you should have no difficulty doing the activity. Once you have completed the basic activity, there are also suggested variations that you can try, now or later. At the end of each activity is an "Afterwords" section to provide additional information.

FLASH
DANCE

FLASH DANCE

1/4 in = .64 cm	2 in = 5.1 cm
1/2 in = 1.27 cm	3 in =7.6 cm
3/4 in =1.9 cm	9 in = 22.9 cm
1 in = 2.54 cm	12 in =30.5 cm
1 1/2 in = 3.8 cm	16 in =40.6 cm

Put on your dancing shoes — it's time to *boogie!* All you need is a strobe to light up your life and help you catch all the flashiest action! It should take about 30 minutes to make.

YOU WILL NEED

Empty cardboard box, about 16″ by 16″ by 9″ or at least 2″ narrower than the length of your drill and bit

Pencil and compass for drawing a circle

Utility knife

Crank-type hand drill with ¼″ drill bit

Piece of cardboard from another box, 12″ by 12″

Scissors

Jumbo-size drinking straw

Masking tape

Ruler

Bright flashlight

Bicycle (optional)

Have you ever seen people dancing in the light of a flashing strobe? Their movements look jerky — like they're moving in slow motion. With a stroboscope, you can create all kinds of special visual effects. You can even make drops of water seem to *stop* in midair! Just get ready…turn out the lights…and do the Flash Dance!

1 To make your stroboscope, or strobe light, you will need to cut several holes in two sides of your cardboard box. Use the two biggest sides of the box and consider one side the "front" and the other the "back."

First, make a small hole with the point of your pencil in the front of the box. Position the hole about 3″ down from the top of the box, and centered between the corners. Then use a utility knife or scissors to cut a vertical opening in the *back* of the box, opposite the pencil hole. This vertical slash should start at the top of the box and be about 3″ long. Make the opening 1½″ wide — or wide enough so that the handle of your drill can sit in the space you've made. Be sure to center the slash between the corners of the box. Now you should be able to push the drill bit through the hole in the front, and rest the drill handle in the slash in the back of the box, as shown in the diagram.

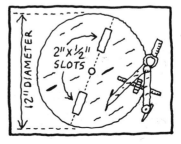

DRILL HANDLE IN SLASH

2 Use a compass to draw a circle 12″ in diameter on the extra piece of cardboard and cut the circle out with scissors. Draw a line across the circle, through the center hole, to mark the diameter. Cut two slots in the disk, on the diameter line, each starting about one inch from the edge of the circle. Each slot should be 2″ long and ½″ wide. With a pencil, poke a hole in the exact center of the disk. Make the hole just big enough to push the drinking straw through.

12″ DIAMETER — 2″ x ½″ SLOTS

3 Cut off a piece of the straw, making it the same length as the drill bit. In one end of the straw, use scissors to cut 4 slashes, each about 1″ long. Now you should be able to bend the four split ends of straw backward, to use as tabs.

4 Push the straw through the hole in the disk, and bend the tabs flat

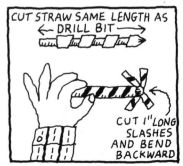

CUT STRAW SAME LENGTH AS ← DRILL BIT →

CUT 1″LONG SLASHES AND BEND BACKWARD

against it. With masking tape, secure the tabs to the face of the disk. Remove the drill bit from the drill, and put the bit inside the straw, with the point of the bit going toward the tabs. Now the drill bit is inside the straw, and the straw is attached to the cardboard disk. Stick the straw-and-bit combo through the hole in the front of the carton. From inside the carton, tighten the straw-and-bit combo in the drill chuck — the place where the drill bit fits into the drill. If you have done this correctly, you will be able to turn the crank on the drill and see the disk spin around.

5 Next you will need to cut a square hole 2" by 2" on the front of the carton. *You must make*

MAKE SURE SLOTS IN DISC WILL PASS OVER HOLE

2" X 2" SQUARE HOLE

FLASHLIGHT

sure that the slots in the disk will pass right over this hole as the disk turns. To mark the place, hold the disk still and make a line on the carton by drawing through one of the slots. Then cut through the mark with the utility knife. Now, working from the inside of the box, enlarge the hole around the cut you just made, so that the hole is 2" square.

6 Another hole must be made in the *back* of the box, exactly opposite the 2" square hole in the front

of the box. Make this last hole just big enough for your flashlight — so that the flashlight can be wedged tightly into the hole. The flashlight should shine directly through the 2" square hole in the front.

7 Now it's showtime! Turn out all the lights, and turn on the flashlight. When you rotate the disk by turning the drill crank, the light will shine out of the front of the box in flashes. The faster you turn the crank, the faster the strobe will flash.

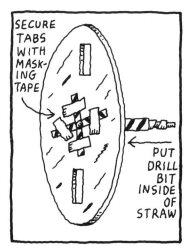

SECURE TABS WITH MASKING TAPE

PUT DRILL BIT INSIDE OF STRAW

ST/87

You may need a friend or two to help you experiment with your strobe. One person can hold the flashlight, to make sure the light is shining straight through the 2" square hole in the front. (Or balance the flashlight on some books set in the box.) Another person can turn the crank on the drill while you try these experiments:

- Put on light-colored clothes and dance in the strobe-light beam! Can you figure out why your movements look jerky?
- Turn on a water faucet so that the water comes out in a thin stream of droplets. Then turn out the lights and shine your flashing strobe at the water. Can you make the drops hang in space? Can you make the drops of water appear to move *upward*?
- Turn your bicycle upside down and spin the front wheel. With all the lights out, shine your strobe at the spinning tire. If you vary the speed of the strobe light, you will be able to make the wheel appear to stop spinning. Can you make it look like the wheel is spinning backward? Can you use your strobe to figure out how fast (how many revolutions per minute) your bicycle tire is spinning?
- Try using a slide projector,

instead of a flashlight, as the light source in your stroboscope. The stronger beam of light will give you more dramatic effects.

AFTERWORDS

Did your stroboscope really make drops of water hang in midair — or were your eyes playing tricks? The answer is: both. Water *does* come out of the faucet drop by drop. But water moves so quickly that normally you can't look at just one drop: Another drop always comes along before you even get a chance to zero in on the first one! They all flow together in your mind, and in fact they all flow together as they come out of the faucet, too.

But — if you turned the crank of your stroboscope at just the right speed, the drop of water you looked at seemed to hang in midair. And as everyone knows, water drops don't do that; what you were really seeing was a series of drops of water. First you saw drop #1 suspended, let's say, about an inch below the faucet. Then the stroboscope turned out the light, and didn't turn it back on again until *another* drop of water — drop #2 — was in that same position!

Then the light went out, and came back on again for drop #3. This created the illusion that one drop was hanging in midair, when really you were seeing many drops, each falling into the exact same position below the faucet.

By turning the crank even faster, perhaps you saw the drops of water appear to move up — back into the faucet! Here's what happened: First you looked at drop #1, an inch below the faucet. Then you look at drop #2, but it was only ¾" below the faucet. When the light came on again, drop #3 had fallen to only ½" below the faucet. Each drop you looked at was closer to the faucet, so the drops appeared to be going backward.

The stroboscope produces fabulous lighting effects, but the stroboscope business would probably flicker and die out if those were the only uses for this fancy flashing light. For instance, did you know that auto mechanics use strobe lights to work on your car engine? They use them to visually stop the action of the crankshaft, which is spinning around rapidly while the motor is running. That way they can check to see if the

engine timing is accurate — in other words, they can make sure that everything is happening at just the right moment to make the car run smoothly.

Strobe lights also let mechanics in other industries view their machinery while it is in operation, to check for defects or to observe parts that might need adjustment. For instance, huge gears in factory equipment may appear to be meshing when the machine is turned off. But under the stress of operation, the gears could be coming together incorrectly. The only way to check it out is to look at the gears while the machine is running. Superstrobe to the rescue!

In the newspaper industry, strobes are used to visually "slow down" the huge rolls of paper that fly across the press. Pressmen can then read the newspapers *while* they are being printed, to make sure that the printing job is right. In the audio equipment industry, strobe lights are used to view the vibrating parts in a loudspeaker. And with flash strobe photography, biologists can record and study such things as the movements of a hummingbird's wings!

NIGHT MOVES

NIGHT MOVES

1 in = 2.54 cm
12 in = 30.5 m
10 ft = 3.1 m
15 ft = 4.6 m

The first game in Night Moves can be played in 30 minutes or less. The second game is enough fun to fill up several hours on a steamy summer night. Just be sure to listen for the screech of a bat or the hoot of an owl whoooo might want to join in your experiment!

YOU WILL NEED

Clean laundry, especially socks
Paper and pen or marker
1 Piece of lightweight cardboard
Tape
Flashlight
Blindfold (optional)
A small empty can

Owls, bats, raccoons, deer, skunks, mice, and porcupines all get around in the dark very well. That's because they're all nocturnal animals, which means that they're up all night and they sleep all day. *You* may live that way sometimes, too—especially in the sum-mer. But that doesn't mean you're really adapted to the night the way nocturnal ani-mals are. For one thing, you don't have the sharp hearing and keen eyesight that noc-turnal animals have. And you probably don't need them. After all, you don't have to fight off vicious animals to get a decent snack during a late-night raid on the refrigerator!

But, hey—why feel inferi-or to these nighttime prowlers when you haven't even tested yourself in the dark? By play-ing these two games and making some Night Moves, you can find out just how dif-ferent you and the wildlife are!

GAME No. 1: SEEING IN THE DARK

1 Have ready a pile of clean, unsorted socks and a few shirts. Turn out all the lights in the room and close the blinds so that just a *little* light from the street comes in.

2 Look around the dark-ened room and talk about which things you can see clearly and which things you cannot see. Can you read a book title in the dark from 12 inches away? Have someone stand on the far side of the room, and hold up a shirt. Can you identify who it belongs to right away? Just wait…your eyes may not have completely adjusted to the dark.

3 Start sorting through the clean socks and take turns deciding what color each sock is. Put all the blue socks in one pile, all the red ones in another pile, and so on. Use the paper and pen or marker to make a sign labeling each pile of socks by color. Do you find yourself holding each sock up very close to your face to see the color better? Why do you think that is?

4 When you're finished sorting the socks, look around the room again. You'll notice that you can see much more now than you could when you'd only been in the dark for five minutes. Can you read the book title now?

5 Turn on the lights and check out the piles of socks. Most likely, you'll find some red socks in the black pile or some gray ones in the beige pile. And you might even find some things that aren't socks in the sock pile! As a matter of fact, maybe you should have a raccoon sort your laundry from now on!

GAME No. 2: HEARING IN THE DARK

1 Use a lightweight piece of cardboard to make a cone with a 1″ open-ing at the small end. Tape the cone over the end of a flashlight. This will narrow the beam of the flashlight so that the light shines on a smaller area.

2 Go outside after dark, or turn out all the lights in your living room, and choose someone to be "It." If you are playing this game outside, try to find a grassy spot to play it in. Have the person who is It sit down on the ground, either blindfolded or with his or her eyes closed, and let him or her hold the flashlight. Place an empty can a few feet behind the person who is It.

3 Have all the other players stand about 10 to 15 feet in front of the person who is It. These players are called the Creepers.

As quietly as possible, the Creepers must try to sneak past the person who is It.

4 Whenever the person who is It hears a Creeper coming, he or she points the flashlight in the direction of the sound and turns it on. Sweeping the flashlight back and forth is not allowed. If the flashlight beam actually shines on the Creeper, the Creeper must say "You got me," and go back to the starting line. But if the light doesn't touch the Creeper, then the Creeper may stay there, remain silent, and creep again. The person who is It should not remove the blindfold or open his or her eyes until the end of the game.

WHAT ARTICLE OF CLOTHING IS THIS?

TURN OUT THE LIGHTS!

CAN A CAT SEE BETTER THAN YOU?

CAN YOU READ THIS BOOK?

#1

NIGHT MOVES

WHAT COLOR IS THIS?

#2

THE FLASHLIGHT

TAPE TO SIDE

CONE OF PAPER WITH 1" OPENING

5 When all the Creepers have made it to the empty can behind the person who is It without getting caught in the flashlight beam, the game is over. Then it is someone else's turn to be It.

VARIATIONS

■ Play the game in a wooded spot; the leaves on bushes and the twigs on the ground will make it much harder to sneak around quietly.

■ Have the person who is It cover one ear during the game. Can he or she still tell where the creeping sounds are coming from? Do you think you need both ears to accurately sense the direction of sounds?

■ Set a limit on the number of times the flashlight may be turned on.

Now that you've played both games, what do you think about nocturnal animals? If you were an animal, would you rather have excellent night vision or terrific hearing?

AFTERWORDS

More than half of the world's animals are active at night. Considering how hard it is to get around in the dark, and how much easier it is to do things in daylight, the big question is: Why? Why are so many animals either nocturnal, which means they are active *only* at night, or arrhythmic (without rhythm), which means they can be just as active at night as they are in the daytime? Scientists believe the answer to that question has to do with the relationship between the predatory, or "hunting," animals and the animals that are their prey, the "hunted."

Here's how the theory goes. Long ago, when the animals we know today were first evolving, the prey animals found that if they wandered around in the daytime looking for food, they were easily seen by the predators, who quickly attacked. So the prey animals remained still during the day, whether they were sleeping or not. When the protective night came, they went looking for food. But in the dark, the animals needed excellent night vision and superior hearing to find a decent meal for themselves and still avoid becoming someone else's dinner. Within each species, a few animals *did* have superior senses and they survived the longest, passing their traits along to their offspring. Meanwhile, the predatory animals were staying up at night, too, and over time they developed the same good hearing and night vision as well. So they're all back to where they started!

With many animals, you can tell just by looking at them whether they have good night vision, supersensitive hearing, or both. All you have to do is observe the size of their ears and eyes. Big ears, which cup forward like a bell or a horn, "catch" more sound waves and direct them down into the animal's inner ear. Big eyes allow more light to enter the eye and strike a light-sensitive membrane called the retina. But even animals with small ears or small eyes can often see and hear better than people can, because the internal structure of their sense organs is so highly developed.

Consider the difference between a nocturnal animal's retina and yours, for example.

Both types of retinas are made up of two different kinds of cells that can receive light. These cells are called *rods* and *cones*. Because they are much more sensitive to light, rods function in the dark or at night. Cones function during the day or in bright light because they are less sensitive. But a nocturnal animal's retina has many more rods than yours does. There may be as many as one million tightly packed rods to every $\frac{1}{25}$ of an inch of retina! That's why most nocturnal animals can see things in the dark that people aren't ever aware of.

But even if you had as many rods in your retina as an animal does, you still wouldn't be able to see colors in the dark. That's because rods aren't sensitive to color at all. Only cones are sensitive to color. When you played Night Moves, you weren't supposed to be able to sort the socks correctly—and if you *could,* it's because you had enough light in the room to stimulate the cones in your retina.

COLOR & LIGHT

COLOR & LIGHT

Roses are red,
Violets are blue,
We have a Color
Activity for you!
You'll need about 45 minutes
to make and experiment
with color wheels.

YOU WILL NEED

3 Flashlights
Balloons in four colors: red,
    yellow, green, and blue
Scissors
Heavy white paper
Compass for drawing circles
Ruler and pencil
Crayons or felt-tip markers in
    all colors
Hand-cranked drill and
    drill bit

Note: If you don't have a
hand drill, you can spin your
color wheels with a piece of
string as shown on page 16.

What color is white? Most
people think that white is *no
color.* But the truth is that
white is the color you see
when *all* the colors of the
rainbow are reflected at
once. You can trick your eyes
(and brain) into seeing white
by looking at all of the rainbow colors at the exact
same time. If the colors are
spinning around so fast that
you can't really see them
separately, your brain will put
them together and see white.
Try it and *see!*

1 Is white light really
white? Or is it made
up of many different
colors? To find out, try mix-
ing colored lights and see
what you get. With the scissors, cut the necks off of
some colored balloons.
Stretch a red balloon across
one flashlight so that it makes
red light. Stretch a yellow or
green balloon across another
flashlight, and a blue balloon
across the third flashlight.
Turn out the room lights and
shine the red light at a white
wall or white piece of paper.
Do you see a red spot? Now
shine the blue flashlight at
the same spot, so that it
overlaps the red. What color
do you see? Add a third
color—either yellow or
green—from a third flash-
light. Which three colors
mixed together make the
spot appear to be white?

2 Make a color wheel
with all the colors of
the rainbow. Use a
compass to draw a circle
about 3½" in diameter on
heavy white paper. With a
ruler and a pencil, divide the
circle into eight equal pie-
shaped sections. Color each
section a different color,
starting with red and then
adding orange, yellow, green,
blue, indigo, and violet.
Leave the last section white.
Cut out your colored circle.
Carefully poke the end of the
drill bit through the center of
the color wheel. Don't make
a big hole in the paper, or it
won't spin on the drill. Stand
in front of a mirror, with the
color wheel facing it, and
turn the crank handle of the
drill as fast as you can. Do
you see all the colors separately—or does your brain
combine them to make an-
other color? (If you don't see
a pure white, it's probably
because you've colored
one section darker than the
others.)

3 Do you think that the
colors on the wheel
are just spinning so
fast that *any* combination of
colors would look like
white? That's not the case,
and you can prove it to
yourself by making another
color wheel. But this time,
make one half of the wheel
red and the other half blue,
and spin it on the drill. What
do you see? Even though
this color wheel is spinning
just as fast as the other one,
your brain can see the two
separate colors flashing by.

4 Make a color wheel that *will* allow your brain to combine the two colors. Divide the wheel into eight sections. Color every other section red. Color the alternate pie shapes blue. When you spin this disk, what color do you see? Make another color wheel using alternating orange and blue sections...or red and green...or purple and yellow. Look at the Color Combos chart to the right. Can you figure out why these combinations will make you see white?

COLOR COMBOS

There are only three *primary* colors: red, yellow, and blue. You can combine the primary colors to make other colors, called *secondary* colors. But if you combine *all* the primary colors, using light beams, you will get white light.

Primary	Secondary
Red + Blue	= Purple
Red + Yellow	= Orange
Blue + Yellow	= Green

5 Make a Fetchner wheel like the one shown here. The easiest way to do it is to use a compass. Hold the point of the compass in the center of the circle the whole time.

Draw a curved segment, then close the compass a little bit (in other words, move the pencil closer to the point) and draw another curved segment. Continue drawing curves and then closing the compass a little until you have copied the Fetchner wheel. Make the lines dark using a black felt-tipped pen or crayon. Be sure that you can see the white spaces between the curved lines.

Spin the Fetchner wheel *at a moderate speed* using the hand-crank drill. Don't spin it too fast. Do you see some thin lines of color? Spin the wheel in the op-

1.

2. CUT OFF NECK AND STRETCH ON FLASHLIGHT

posite direction and you will see different colors. This is an unexplained phenomena—scientists don't really understand why it works!

HOW TO SPIN A COLOR WHEEL WITH A STRING

Use a piece of string that's about 4 feet long. Poke two holes in the color wheel, one on each side of the center point. The two holes should be about ¾" apart. Thread the string through the holes, as shown, and tie the ends together. Hold one end in each hand. Put a twist in the string by spinning the color wheel around and around in a jump-rope motion, as shown. Then pull outward on both ends of the string quickly and tightly. The string will untwist, and that will make the color wheel spin. Watch it while it spins, to see what color it makes.

TWIRL WHEEL LIKE JUMP-ROPE   THEN PULL STRING

AFTERWORDS

If you've ever seen a rainbow or the colors reflected from light shining through a prism, you know that white light is made up of many colors called a spectrum. Early scientists had observed this also, but Sir Isaac Newton was the first one to understand that if these colors could be separated by a prism, they could also be recombined by a lens or prism to make white light again.

Later, scientists discovered that each color of light in the spectrum has a different temperature. By placing a thermometer in the space just below the red part of the spectrum—a space that looks dark to us because we can't see the light there— scientists were able to discover some invisible light called *infrared* light. They knew it was there because it gave off some heat! Similarly, the space above the violet area gave off heat too. So scientists knew there was invisible light *above* the violet—*ultraviolet* light.

If light is like a wave, the light "waves" from each color of light would be different lengths. Ultraviolet waves are much shorter than infrared. The shorter waves are sent out at a much higher frequency than the longer ones. Therefore, ultraviolet light has more energy than infrared. In fact, the ultraviolet rays from the sun have enough energy to give you a sunburn!

Infrared is a lower energy light wave, very similar to a radio wave. These waves are often used to make lasers. A laser is a beam of light in which the waves are all exactly the same length, and, more importantly, they are all *in phase*—moving along together, like people in a marching band marching in step. This is called *coherent* light. When a beam of coherent light is focused into a laser beam, the energy and light is concentrated in a way that regular light rays are not.

In the spectrum, red has the longest wave length and the lowest energy, and violet has the shortest and highest. As you go through the colors in the rainbow—red, orange, yellow, green, blue, indigo, violet—each subsequent color has more energy.

Did you know that an object's "color" is really the result of which color of light is *reflected*? Take a red apple, for instance. White light, containing all the colors, falls on the apple, but most of the colors are absorbed. Only the red part of the spectrum is reflected, so you see the apple as red. But the apple doesn't have any "red" in it.

But why does the sky look blue? In outer space, the sky looks almost black, because there is no atmosphere—no dust or gas—to reflect the light rays from the sun. But earth's atmosphere is composed of dust, gases, and drops of water, which are able to scatter and reflect *some* of the light from the sun. Because of the wave lengths of each color of light, it is the blue light that is scattered most easily. So we see the sky as blue. At sunset, however, we often see the sky as red, orange, or pink. That's partly because the dust in the atmosphere is denser near the earth. The dust scatters the blue, leaving the red and orange light waves, to give us a beautiful sunset.

STAR TRACKING

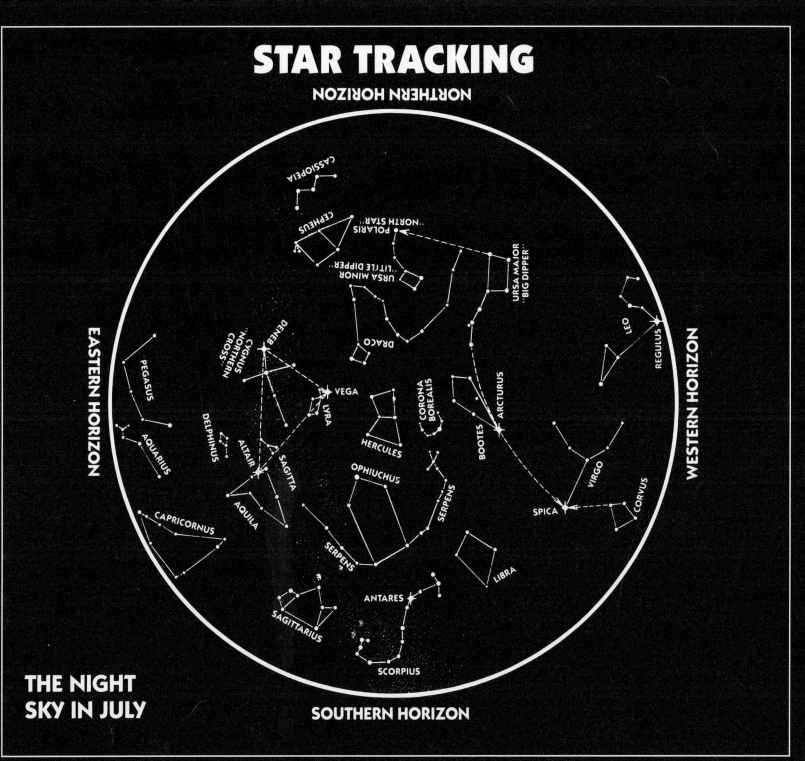

NORTHERN HORIZON

CASSIOPEIA

CEPHEUS

POLARIS "NORTH STAR"

URSA MINOR "LITTLE DIPPER"

URSA MAJOR "BIG DIPPER"

DRACO

DENEB

CYGNUS "NORTHERN CROSS"

VEGA

LYRA

PEGASUS

CORONA BOREALIS

ARCTURUS

LEO

REGULUS

DELPHINUS

ALTAIR

SAGITTA

HERCULES

BOOTES

AQUILA

OPHIUCHUS

SERPENS

VIRGO

SPICA

CORVUS

AQUARIUS

CAPRICORNUS

SERPENS

LIBRA

SAGITTARIUS

ANTARES

SCORPIUS

EASTERN HORIZON

WESTERN HORIZON

THE NIGHT SKY IN JULY

SOUTHERN HORIZON

17

STAR TRACKING

1/2 in = 1.27 cm
1 C = .24 l
1 1/4 C = .3 l   1/2 tsp = 2.5 ml
1 1/2 C = .36 l   2 tsp = 10 ml
1 1/2 tsp = 7.5 ml 3 T = 45 ml

Be different! Look at the stars in the *daytime*, instead of at night. With these experiments, you can put on your own light show, make a delicious breakfast, and learn how to identify some constellations at the same time!

A sky full of twinkling stars is a wonderful thing to watch. But most people agree that it's hard to find the constellations in the night sky. Part of the problem is that constellations don't look anything like the names given to them. Sagittarius, for instance, is supposed to be an archer; but, as you can see on the star map on page 17, Sagittarius looks more like a tea kettle with a triangular spout. And to make it even harder, there aren't any lines drawn in the sky to point out the shape.

Once you become familiar with their patterns, though, the constellations will be easier to spot. Try picking

out the patterns in these star-studded pancakes, and then go on to make your own super-star light show. By the time you finish these experiments, your star-gazing skills will be super-sharp!

EXPERIMENT NO. 1 — STELLAR PANCAKES

Learn to recognize Sagittarius in a blueberry pancake, and you'll have no trouble seeing the archer in the night sky. You'll need about 60 minutes to make and eat the pancakes and talk about the stars.

YOU WILL NEED

Pancake mix, or prepare the
    recipe at right
1 Cup fresh blueberries or
    raisins
Griddle or frying pan
Stove
map of the night sky
    (see page 17)
Spatula

186,000 mi = 299,274 km
8 in to 10 in = 20.3 cm to 25.4 cm

1 Make the pancake batter, using a box mix or the recipe below. Have ready 1 cup of washed blueberries or 1 cup of raisins. While you are making the batter, let the other people in your family look at the map of the night sky.

PANCAKE RECIPE

1 Egg
1¼ Cups milk
3 Tablespoons melted butter
1½ Cups flour
1½ Teaspoons baking powder
½ Teaspoon salt
2 Tablespoons sugar

Beat egg. Add milk and butter. Stir in flour, baking powder, salt, and sugar; mix until the batter is almost smooth.
    Yield: Makes 10 eight- to 10-inch pancakes.

2 Grease a griddle or frying pan (or use one with a non stick coating). Heat it on the stove until a drop of water skips across the surface. Now you know the pan is hot enough.

3 Pour enough batter onto the griddle to make an 8- to 10-inch pancake. Then choose one constellation from the map of the night sky. Arrange blueberries or raisins in the pancake to resemble the pattern of the stars in that constellation.

4 When bubbles appear on top of pancake, use a spatula to turn the pancake over. Cook the other side until golden brown.

5 Continue making pancakes, using a different constellation for each one, until you have one or two pancakes for each person in your family. Then serve the pancakes and put the map of the night sky in the center of the table. Each person should try to identify the constellation in his or her pancake before eating it!

EXPERIMENT No. 2— STARS ON THE CEILING

Here's another great way to practice identifying the

constellations, one at a time. In about 30 minutes, you can make your own private planetarium.

YOU WILL NEED

Empty round oatmeal box
Scissors, tape, ruler
Flashlight
Cardboard
Map of the night sky
Pencil
1 Nail
Red cellophane

1 Cut a small hole in the bottom end of an empty oatmeal box and put a flashlight through the hole, taping around the edges to hold the flashlight in place. Remove the box lid and cut a circular hole in it, leaving a ½" rim all around.

2 Use cardboard or very thick paper to cut out several disks that are the same size as the *outside* dimension of the oatmeal box lid. These disks will be

the "slides" you'll put on the oatmeal box, which is your "constellation projector."

3 Using the star map as a guide, draw one constellation on each of the cardboard disks. Make nail holes where each star in the constellation appears.

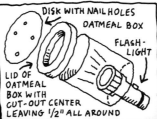

DISK WITH NAIL HOLES
OATMEAL BOX
FLASH-LIGHT
LID OF OATMEAL BOX WITH CUT-OUT CENTER LEAVING ½" ALL AROUND

4 Now put the lid back on the oatmeal box and point the flashlight upward. Turn out the lights, and take turns projecting your constellations on the ceiling by placing your disks *on top* of the cutout lid. The flashlight will shine through the nail holes you've made, and the dots of light will form the shape of the constellation on the ceiling. You may want to make a game out of this, by saying that the first person

to identify your constellation correctly takes over the oatmeal box and gets to project his or her favorite constellation next.

STAR-GAZING STRATEGY

Now that you've had some practice identifying the constellations, you're ready to go outside to gaze at the star-studded sky.

■ Sit or lie down. You'll get bored and tired if you stand.

■ Remember that the patterns you're looking for are *much* larger in the sky than they were on the pancakes or on your ceiling.

■ Cover the end of a flashlight with red cellophane, and use this to look at the star map when you're outside. Because of the cellophane, your eyes won't have to constantly adjust from a bright light to the dark of the night sky.

■ Be patient. Your eyes will adjust to the dark in 5 or 6 minutes, but your night vision will *continue* to improve. In 30 to 45 minutes, you'll be able to see even more stars than you could after only 5 minutes. The longer you watch the sky, the more stars you'll see.

AFTERWORDS

Look at the constellations at different times of the night. You'll notice that some of them seem to move across the sky, "rising" and "setting" like the sun. Actually, the Earth's rotation is responsible for this illusion. As the Earth spins, stars that were below the horizon at the beginning of the evening come into view a few hours later. However, one star — Polaris, the North Star — remains in the same spot all night, and the constellations surrounding it are always visible. That's because Polaris is directly above the North Pole. You can easily find Polaris: If you can spot the Big Dipper, the two stars along the outer edge of Big Dipper's "bowl" point to it. (See the star map.)

Another change in the night sky results from the Earth's other movement — its revolution around the sun. In summer, certain constellations that earlier this year were above the horizon only during the daylight hours are now above the horizon at night. For instance, Leo the Lion can be seen in the evening all summer; but by the end of August, Leo will have dropped out of sight. At about the

same time, Pegasus will become visible in the evening for the first time this year.

Although we don't usually think of it as a star, the nearest star to the Earth is actually the sun. If we could look at the sun from billions of miles away, it would look just like the other stars overhead. It would no longer be the brightest star in the sky, but it wouldn't be the *dimmest* one either.

After the sun, the next closest star to the Earth is named Alpha Centauri. It is 4.3 light-years away, which means that if we could travel 186,000 miles per *second* — which is the speed of light — it would *still* take us 4.3 years to get there! Even though it's nearby, Alpha Centauri isn't bright enough to be seen. The nearest star we *can* see is Sirius, located in the constellation Canis Major. Sirius is the brightest star in the sky. It becomes visible again in December.

One of the most beautiful and brightest objects in the sky, known as the "evening star," isn't really a star at all. It's Venus, the wandering planet, and you can find it in July in the west just after sunset, or in the east just before sunrise.

Other planets may also be visible to the naked eye, if you know where to look. Mars can be found in Sagittarius and Jupiter should be visible somewhere between Pisces and Aquarius. The trick to finding them is to become familiar with the constellations, so that you'll know when there's an extra "star" stuck in there where it shouldn't be. Remember that the planets look just like stars — except that Mars and Jupiter are not as bright as some stars are. Also, planets *don't twinkle*.

Although we can see between 2,000 and 3,000 individual stars, that's nothing compared with the 100,000 stars in our galaxy, the Milky Way. Most of those stars are too far away to be seen without a telescope. They all seem to blend together into a misty band, which, in July, runs through the constellations of Cassiopeia, Cygnus, and Scorpius. And this blend of stars is only *one* galaxy — one little neighborhood — among the universe of maybe 2,500 galaxies or more.

CAMERA CREATIONS

CAMERA CREATIONS

Put together your own photography studio and see what develops! This activity should take you about 45 minutes to complete.

YOU WILL NEED

1 Empty round oatmeal box
Black spray paint or
    poster paint
Sharp knife
Small piece of aluminum foil
Tape, scissors, needle
2 Pencils, 1 pen
2 Red balloons
Flashlight
Package of 5" by 7" single-
    weight photographic
    paper, #1 or #2
    (see Note)
Wristwatch with a
    second hand

Important: *You will also need all of the darkroom supplies listed on page 23.*

Note: All photographic supplies are inexpensive and readily available at camera stores and photography shops. Do not open the photographic paper until you reach Step 6!

Believe it or not, you can actually make a camera by simply putting a tiny pinhole in one end of a light-tight box. That's how the earliest cameras worked! You'll be amazed at the sharp quality of the pictures taken with an empty oatmeal box.

1 Paint the inside of an empty oatmeal box with black spray paint or poster paint. Do the same to the inside of the lid.

2 Use a sharp knife to cut a circle about 1½" in diameter out of the *center* of the bottom of the box. Save the cardboard circle, because you'll need to use it later: It will be the "lens cap" for your camera.

3 Cut a square piece of aluminum foil slightly larger than the hole you made in the bottom of the box. Tape the foil to the *inside* of the box so that it covers the hole. Be sure to keep the foil smooth, and tape around all four sides of the foil

PAINT INSIDE OF BOX WITH BLACK PAINT
OATM
1½"
ALUMINUM WITH PINHOLE

square so that no light can get through. Now use a needle to make a pinhole in the aluminum foil in the *exact center* of the bottom of the box. The hole should be just a pinhole **— no larger.**

4 Fit the cardboard "lens cap" back into place and tape it so that it can be opened like a flap or door. Tape a pencil along the outside of the oatmeal box, and tape another pencil parallel to the first one, about 2" away from it.

TAPE PENCILS TO BOX
M
TAPE "LENS CAP" SO THAT IT CAN OPEN LIKE A FLAP

5 Before you can load your camera, you need to make a "safelight" — a dark-red light that won't ruin the photographic paper when turned on in a completely blackened room. To make a safelight, cut off and discard the "necks" from two red balloons. Stretch the remaining pieces of balloon across the end of a flashlight, one on top of the other, like a double pair of socks.

STRETCH BALLOON ACROSS END OF FLASHLIGHT LIKE A PAIR OF SOCKS
CUT OFF ENDS

6 Take your safelight, oatmeal-box camera, scissors, tape, and unopened pack of photographic paper into a *completely* dark closet or bathroom. It is best to do this step at night and turn out all the lights in your house, so that *no* light will leak in through the cracks around the windows and doors. Turn on your red flashlight. Remove the lid from the oatmeal box; make three tape loops (sticky-side out) and set them in the lid. Now you may open your package of photographic paper. You will see that the photographic paper is wrapped in a black paper liner or envelope, inside the cardboard package. Always keep the photo paper inside the black paper envelope and keep the black envelope inside the cardboard package. **Also remember:** *Never* turn on the room lights until the photographic paper is put back in its package.

7 Take out only one sheet of photographic paper and cut a circular piece to fit inside the oatmeal box lid. The smoother, shinier side of the paper is called the emulsion side. Put the circle of paper in the lid with the emulsion side facing up. Press it flat; the tape loops in the lid will hold it in place. Put the lid on the box tightly, and your camera is loaded!

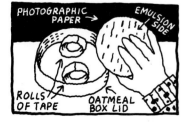

PHOTOGRAPHIC PAPER → EMULSION SIDE

ROLLS OF TAPE   OATMEAL BOX LID

8 Go outside the next day and set your camera on something solid. The pencils along the sides of the box will keep your camera from rolling. If it's windy, you might also need to steady the box by putting one hand firmly on top. Point the camera at whatever you want to photograph, and open the lens cap. Leave the lens cap open for 1 minute if you are photographing in very bright sunlight, 2 minutes on a somewhat cloudy day, or 3 minutes if it is very overcast outside. (**Note:** You may need to experiment with the exposure times. A one-minute exposure on a bright, sunny day works best.) While the lens cap is open, you must not move the camera!

Jot down a description of the subject matter you photograph each day. Also write down the exposure times — the number of minutes and seconds you had the lens cap open. Later, when you develop the pictures, you can look at these notes to find out which exposure times worked best.

9 At night, go into your darkroom with the red flashlight and remove the exposed circle of paper from the camera lid. *Put it back in the package of photographic paper.* Cut another circle and reload your camera. After taking 7 or 8 pictures, you willl be ready to develop them.

HINTS FOR SUCCESS:

■ Take pictures of things that stand still. If you want to photograph people, they will have to remain absolutely still for 1 to 3 minutes.

■ If your pictures come out completely black, your camera may have a leak. Make sure the lid fits tightly and use shorter exposure times.

■ When loading your camera, **do not** cut out extra circles of photographic paper in advance. Otherwise, you won't be able to tell which ones are exposed and which ones are unexposed.

1 1/2 in = 3.8 cm
2 in = 5.1 cm
5 in = 12.7 cm
7 in = 17.8 cm
4 ft = 1.2 m
1 tsp = 5 ml
1 1/2 qt = 1.4 l
68° F = 20° C

DARKROOM INSTRUCTIONS FOR PINHOLE CAMERA

This activity is best done at night, when you can make your kitchen or bathroom *completely* dark.

YOU WILL NEED

1 Small package of Dektol paper developer
Measuring cup
Long-handled spoon for stirring
3 large glass or plastic bowls, each with at least 1-1/2-quart capacity
Water
1 Teaspoon white vinegar
1 Small package of photographic fixative
Sink
Tongs
Photographic paper, wristwatch, and safelight from camera activity
Paper towels
5" by 7" Sheet of glass or Plexiglass
Sponge for cleanup
Note: All darkroom work should be done with water and chemicals at 68°F. When you mix the chemicals, you can judge the water temperature by feel. At 68°F, it will feel very cool, but not ice-

cold. The water should not feel warm at all.

Caution: Photographic chemicals can stain your clothing and are irritating to the skin. Avoid touching the developer and fixative. Wash any spills with clear water. You can also protect the floor from spills by using newspaper or a plastic dropcloth.

■ Mix the Dektol developer according to the directions on the package and pour it into a large glass bowl. Half fill another bowl with water and add 1 teaspoon of white vinegar to it. This second bowl is called the "stop bath." In a third bowl, mix the photographic fixative according to the directions on the package. Place these bowls in a kitchen or bathroom. Choose a room that can be made completely dark. The bowls should be lined up from left to right: first, developer; then, stop bath; then, fixative. Partially fill the sink with water.

■ Make the room *completely* dark except for the red safelight. Have your wristwatch, tongs, paper towels, and photographic paper ready. Open the package of paper and take out just one of the circles that have been exposed in your camera. Slip it into the bowl of developer with the emulsion side facing up, so you can see what's happening as it develops. Rock the bowl gently every 10 seconds. Very soon, you will see a picture starting to appear. Let the picture develop fully; it should take anywhere from 30 seconds to 2 minutes. Don't let the picture turn black.

■ When the picture looks right, use the tongs to remove it from the developer and drop the picture into the stop bath. After 10 seconds, lift the picture out of the stop bath and *drop* it into the fixative. Rock the fixative bowl gently every once in a while. Let the picture sit in the fixative for 5 to 10 minutes. (It is all right to turn the room light on after the picture has been in the fixative for 2 minutes.) Then put it in a sink of cool water for 15 to 30 minutes to rinse.

Important: *Rinse the tongs off in plain water before you develop another picture.* You must never get any of the fixative or stop bath into the developer.

■ While the first picture is fixing, you can go on to develop others. Always work from left to right . . . from developer to stop bath to fixative to the washing sink. When all of the pictures are washed, dry them between two paper towels. You can speed up the drying by resting them over a warm light or near a heater.

   You will notice that your pictures look strange. Everything that should be dark is light and vice versa. This is actually a paper negative — just like the film negatives from a regular camera. Now you can print a paper positive from this paper negative.

■ When the paper negatives are dry, go back into the darkroom. Take with you a small sheet of glass or Plexiglass. Tape the edges of the glass so you don't cut yourself. In the darkroom, with only the red light on, put a new piece of photographic paper on the countertop or some other flat surface. The shiny emulsion side of the paper should be facing up. Put a dry paper negative *face down* on top of the photographic paper. Put the sheet of glass on top of both to hold them tightly together. Make sure that *all* other photo paper is closed up in its package. Now flick the room light on, then off very quickly, just once. It should be on for only about one second — or less. Develop, fix, wash, and dry the new piece of photographic paper just as you developed the paper negatives. If your exposure was right, you will have a positive picture of the scene you photographed earlier in the week.

HINTS FOR SUCCESS:

■ Never turn on the room light until you have checked to be sure that all the photographic paper is properly put away.

■ Keep the red flashlight at least 4 feet away from the photographic paper. Even this safelight can "fog" the paper after a while. Keep the paper closed up tightly in its package except when you are actually using it.

CABBAGE CAPERS

CABBAGE CAPERS

If you're a kitchen chemist, you can perform the magic trick of changing purple water to red or blue! These Cabbage Capers will only take you 30 minutes, and you can make the cabbage into a salad when you're through.

YOU WILL NEED

½ Red cabbage
Sharp knife
2 Large bowls
Colander or strainer
2 Small drinking glasses
Water
Lemon juice
Baking soda
Several test foods, such as orange juice, apple juice, tomato, vegetable soup broth, egg white, cola, cream of tartar, cocoa, salt water, vinegar, tea, etc.

When foods taste sour, it's usually because they contain some kind of acid. Lemon juice is a perfect example of an acid food — the citric acid gives it a very sour taste. The opposite of an acid is called a *base*.

Bases — baking soda, for example — often taste bitter. Foods that are neither acid or base are called *neutral*.

Who cares about acids and bases? You do, when you're sick or have an upset stomach, because acidic foods can irritate your stomach even more. And people who have stomach ulcers also have to watch what they eat; acid can make their ulcers worse. You can find out which foods are acids and which are bases by doing the Cabbage Capers in this colorful experiment!

1 Cut a red cabbage into thin slices and chop the slices into fine pieces, about the size used in cole slaw. Put the chopped cabbage in a large bowl and add 2 cups of very hot tap water. Stir it up and let stand for 15 to 20 minutes, or until the water turns purple. As you can see, *red* cabbage is actually purple, and the water will be a purplish blue.

2 Separate the purple water from the cabbage by pouring the mixture through a strainer or colander into another bowl. This purple water is called an *indicator*. It will change colors to indicate whether various foods are acids or bases. Save the chopped cabbage to make Confetti Coleslaw with the recipe on the next page.

3 Now you're ready to begin doing some kitchen chemistry. Put a tablespoonful of the indicator in a clean glass. Add a few drops of lemon juice. What color did the indicator water change to? Lemon juice is an acid, so now you know what color to expect when you are testing for acids. Don't pour the lemon juice test out yet. You'll need it in the next step.

4 Put a tablespoonful of the indicator in the second glass and add a pinch of baking soda. Baking soda is a base. What color did the indicator change to this

time? All bases will have the same effect on the indicator. Now mix the baking soda test together with the lemon juice test. What color did you get this time? Taste the mixture to see what effect the acid and base had on each other.

Caution: It's okay to taste the foods in this experiment, but do not taste the chemicals tested in the variations below. Tasting is not a safe way to test for acids and bases.

5 Rinse out the glasses well, and continue to test some other foods for acid or base. Remember that if the indicator doesn't change color at all, the food is neutral. Use only a tablespoonful of indicator for each test. For dry foods like cocoa, mix a small amount in water before testing it.

VARIATIONS

■ Collect some water from a local stream, river, or lake. Bring it home and prepare a fresh batch of red-cabbage indicator. Test the water. If the

indicator shows that the water has an acidity or basicity, it probably means that certain bugs, plants, and fish cannot survive in those waters.

■ Make your own litmus paper by cutting white blotting paper into strips and soaking the strips in a fresh batch of dark purple indicator. After the strips have dried, you can use them to test for acid or base by dipping them into various liquids. Take them with you whenever you are going to be near a fresh water supply, and check up on the environment.

■ Test some things that are not foods, like laundry detergent, ammonia, milk of magnesia, soil from your plants or garden, your saliva, and your shampoo. Do you think acids and bases are always good or bad for the environment?

CONFETTI COLESLAW

½ Red cabbage
1 Carrot
1 Green pepper
½ Onion
Lemon juice
½ Cup plain yogurt
½ Cup mayonnaise
½ Teaspoon celery seeds
1 Teaspoon caraway seeds
Salt and pepper to taste

Chop all vegetables into small pieces. Mix the lemon juice, yogurt, and mayonnaise together, and pour over the chopped salad. Add celery seeds, caraway seeds, salt, and pepper ; toss lightly.

AFTERWORDS

In Cabbage Capers, you tested foods for acids and bases. But many substances other than foods are acids and bases (or *alkalis,* as bases are called when they are dissolved in water). You've probably heard of the well-known dangerous acids like hydrochloric acid, which can dissolve metal. But did you know that the poison in a bee sting is a kind of acid too? As with other acids, the bee sting can be neutralized with a common alkali such as baking soda and water. Stinging red ants, car battery fluid, fertilizer, vitamin C, and aspirin all contain acids as well.

Don't put baking soda on a wasp sting, though, because wasp stings are *not* acids — they're alkalis. Some alkalis are just as dangerous as acids, which helps to point out why *all* chemicals should be handled very carefully. Other alkalis include ammonia, Pepto Bismol, the lye used to make soap, and a chemical com-

pound called lithium hydroxide, which was sent along on the Apollo space missions because it has the ability to absorb the carbon dioxide the astronauts exhaled.

The primary characteristics of acids are that they taste sour (but you *should not* taste any chemicals other than foods), they react chemically with metals to produce hydrogen, they change the color of blue litmus paper to red, and they neutralize bases. Bases, on the other hand, taste bitter (again, don't taste chemicals!), they feel slippery or soapy, turn red litmus paper blue, and neutralize acids.

When you made a batch of red cabbage indicator and used it to test for acids and bases, you made one big assumption about the water used in the experiment. You assumed that the water was neutral, not acid or base. If you tested treated water from a city or town water supply, that assumption is probably correct. But although water is considered to be neutral in the world of chemistry, the water you drink doesn't always start out that way.

Imagine the waters that come from upland rivers or streams, or waters that started

out as melted snow at the top of a mountain. Fresh mountain water is practically a synonym for good-tasting water, clean and pure and unpolluted. But are mountain waters neutral? Not necessarily. They often have a slightly acid content, due to the small plants and animals in a river or stream that produce acids as they eat, die, and decay. These acids are not by themselves a sign of pollution.

As the mountain water runs downhill, through the ground and over a great number of limestone rocks, it picks up minerals along the way that make the water more base. Water with a high mineral content is often called "hard" water, and it never tastes as good as the "soft" water from farther uphill. Hard water isn't necessarily polluted, either. As it moves into the big rivers near heavily populated areas, the chances of pollution increase. That's because untreated or inadequately treated sewage water is sometimes put back into the rivers. In any case, the water you finally drink is close to neutral, not because it started out that way, but because it is treated with chemicals to correct the acid or alkali content it originally had.

PIGMENT PIZAZZ

PIGMENT PIZAZZ

Pigment Pizazz takes about an hour to complete. It is most successful when Boston fern or Wandering Jew plant trimmings are used.

YOU WILL NEED

Handful of plant trimmings
1- to 2-Quart stainless steel
    or enamel pot with lid
Clear drinking glass
Stainless steel or plastic spoon
Scissors, stove, strainer, water
As many of these "chemicals" as you have in your kitchen: baking powder, baking soda, citric acid, clear soft drink, cream of tartar, orange juice, onion juice, pickle juice, salt, sugar, and vinegar

There is more color to a plant than meets the eye—more than the greens and browns of its leaves, stems, and roots. Hidden beneath a rich, green disguise, plant pigments of many colors live inside plants. Pigments are the colored substances that help plants absorb light. You can release some of them by gently simmering a few leaves in water. Add a pinch or two of kitchen chemicals and watch those pigments pizazz.

BEFORE YOU START: Picking a Plant

Choose a plant that needs trimming. If you have no plants, get trimmings from the plant of a friend or relative. If you have never trimmed a plant before, get help from someone who has. Trimming should encourage plant growth, not kill the plant. Get trimmings from these plants:

Wandering Jew (*Zebrina pendula* and other varieties)

Boston fern (*Nephrolepsis exaltata*)

Coleus (*Coleus spp.*)

Swedish ivy (*Plectranthus australis*)

Ivy and hairy-leaved plants will not work as well as the other plants. Many other types of plants will work but may be poisonous.

Note: Many plant pigments will stain clothing and wooden or aluminum kitchen tools. Wear an apron to protect your clothing and wash all kitchen tools immediately after using them.

1 Look closely at your plant trimmings. What colors do you see?
■ Use the scissors to cut the trimmings into ½-inch pieces. Put the pieces into the pot.
■ Cover the trimmings with one inch of water. Put the lid on the pot.
■ Gently simmer the trimmings on the stove for about 20 minutes. What color do you think will simmer out of your plant trimmings?

2 While the trimmings are simmering, test your kitchen chemicals. Testing unknown chemicals can be dangerous. These kitchen chemicals are all known foods, so you can smell and taste them without fear.

■ Smell the chemicals and choose the best-smelling one.
■ Taste one of the chemicals. Does it taste sour or bitter? Rinse your mouth with water. Taste another. Pick out the most sour and the most bitter.

3 After 20 minutes, look at your trimmings. Is the color what you expected?
■ Carefully strain the plant juice into a glass. Do not taste this plant juice—it may be poisonous. Also, clean the pot well before using it again.
■ Look at the plant juice. Does your plant have more than just green pigments in its leaves and stems? The color you see comes from other pigments in the leaves and stems.

4 Pour a little plant juice into a couple of cups. Add the best-smelling chemical to the juice in one cup. What happens to the juice?
■ Add the sourest chemical to another cup of juice. What happens? Compare the sweet and sour mixes.

■ Add baking powder to another cup of juice. What happens?

■ Add baking soda to your sourest chemical cup. What is the result?

■ Experiment with the other kitchen chemicals. Can you get the juice to bubble? Make your own colorful combinations.

VARIATION

Make a plant dye by following Pigment Pizazz steps 1 and 3. Just a few trimmings will make enough plant dye to color a handkerchief. After simmering the trimmings, let the juice, or dye, cool.

Drop a handkerchief or wool yarn into the dye. First, tie the fabric into knots to get a tie-dyed effect, if you choose. Stir it around to coat the whole piece evenly. Let it sit in the dye overnight.

In the morning, carefully take your cloth out of the dye and hang it out of direct sunlight to dry.

AFTERWORDS

Green leaves, yellow daffodils, and red tomatoes wouldn't be possible without plant pigments. Neither would many important plant functions. Here is why: Every color absorbs different wavelengths of light. Light energy triggers many different plant functions. For example, chlorophyll, the green pigment in plants, absorbs the light energy that triggers photosynthesis. Photosynthesis is the process by which plants make their own food. Without green pigment, there would be no photosynthesis. Without photosynthesis, plants would starve to death.

Other colors, or pigments, absorb the light energy that makes plants flower. Still others attract bees to spread the pollen necessary to produce new plants. To study the makeup and uses of pigments, scientists perform experiments like Pigment Pizazz. As you have seen, taking the pigments from plants can produce surprising results. The red flower heads of an amaryllis plant produce yellow plant juice, while the red leaves of a weeping cherry tree produce a soft green color. Different parts of the same plant can produce different colors, too. The roots of a cherry tree produce a reddish purple, but its bark produces tans, red, and oranges. Tree bark, onion skins, marigold flowers, cranberries, walnut hulls, and sassafras roots all make dazzling colors and dyes.

Not only can one plant produce many pigments, but many colors can be produced from a single pigment. Metal compounds, acids, and bases can all change the color of plant pigments.

Metal compounds such as alum can brighten or completely change the color of a plant pigment extract. They also help dyes "take" to yarns and fabrics, and prevent fading.

Acids, such as vinegar (acetic acid), will also change the color of plant juice. The white vinegar sold in grocery stores will turn some plant pigments redder. If you don't like the redder color, it can be reversed by adding a base, the opposite of an acid. When the right amount of a base, such as baking soda, is added, the plant juice will return to its original color. Adding even more base may turn the juice greener or bluer.

As you may have observed while performing Pigment Pizazz, acids taste sour and bases taste bitter. But the human tongue is not the most accurate or safe way to test for acids and bases. A more precise and safer way is to use an acid/base or "pH" indicator. Most paper and liquid "pH" indicators originate from plants. Litmus paper, used by chemists, is made from certain plants called lichens. Your kitchen acid/base indicators of vinegar and baking soda are not as sensitive as litmus paper. But even your own Wandering Jew or Boston fern can help you tell that orange juice and black coffee are acidic, while baking soda and milk of magnesia are basic.

HIDDEN RAINBOWS

HIDDEN RAINBOWS

Beautiful sunsets, forest scenes, and colorful rainbows can be found hiding deep in the stroke of your pen. How do you release them for your viewing pleasure? The secret is a technique called *paper chromatography* and will take you less than an hour to discover.

YOU WILL NEED

1 Package of coffee filters
Scissors
Several rubber bands
1 Dishpan, large bowl, or
    other basin at least
    4" deep
Tape
1 Set of colored marking pens,
    water soluble
Old newspaper
1 Set of liquid food colorings,
    small size
Paper plates
Toothpicks
1 Package of M&M candies
Deep-colored fruits and
    vegetables
Vinegar or rubbing alcohol

1/2 in = 1.27 cm
3/4 in = 1.9 cm
4 in = 10.2 cm

1 Cut a bunch of strips of filter paper about ¾" wide and 4" long. Then cut 2 or 3 rubber bands, stretch them across the basin, and tape them in place. Fold one of the paper strips over ½" at the end, and hang it on one of the rubber bands. Put just enough water into the basin to bring the water up to the end of the paper.

2 Select a pen from your set. Use it to draw a line across the width of one of the paper strips, ½" from the bottom. Fold the top of the strip over ½", and hang it on the rubber band. Watch the water wick up the paper, doing its magic on the ink mark as it moves upward.

3 Try all of the colors you can find. Blacks, browns, and dark greens are particularly interesting. Try to find a number of different brands of pens in these dark colors. When the colors have moved as far up the paper as they can (in about 5 minutes), lay them on old newspaper to dry.

VARIATIONS

■ Use your chromatography set-up to find out how food colorings move. Mix drops of food colors on a paper plate to make your own inks, and see if the original colors can be separated out. Use toothpicks to mix the drops of color and to put the marks on the paper strips.

■ Use your set of pens to make many different color marks on paper strips. See what happens when they get absorbed up the paper.

■ Use larger pieces of paper, and draw little pictures and designs on them. Hang them in the basin and watch the modern art unfold.

■ Dip an M&M candy in water, and transfer the color to a strip of paper. Discover the rainbows in the treats you sometimes eat.

■ Test the movement of natural colors, called *pigments*. Try beets, cherries, blueberries, spinach, and other heavily pigmented plants. You can transfer the pigment by putting a little sample of the material on the paper, and smashing the juice onto the paper.

■ Some pigments will not move in water, but might when other solvents are used. Try vinegar (an acid), rubbing alcohol, ammonia or paint thinner. Remember, these solvents should be used with adult supervision, and they are best used outdoors.

AFTERWORDS

While you were having fun discovering hidden rainbows, you were actually dealing with a branch of science called *chromatography.* In Greek, *chroma* meant "color" and *graph* meant "to write." Scientists use this "color writing" to identify different substances.

In your chromatography, you used filter paper, which operates on the principle of *capillarity.* You probably already know that your blood flows through some very small veins called *capillaries.* (Capillary means "tiny tube.")

But where are the tubes in paper? Any paper is made up of tiny fibers that are pressed close together. There are spaces between these fibers that can act like tiny tubes. Suppose you had two walls of fibers and you put them very close together (closer than you can see without a microscope). A water droplet sitting between these two walls would look like this:

You can see that the sides of the droplet are pulled *up* against the walls and the top of the droplet is curved *down.* Two sets of forces are at work here. *Cohesive* forces within the droplet are working between the water molecules to keep the droplet together. At the same time, *adhesive* forces in the paper fibers try to pull, or absorb, the water molecules up into the walls. It's like a tug-of-war!

As long as the adhesive forces are stronger, the water will wet the walls. This means that water will be pulled up the fiber tubes by a process called *capillary action.* When the cohesive forces between the water molecules becomes equal to the adhesive forces between the water and the fiber walls, the water stops rising up the paper.

Next, think of the last time you saw a rain spout on the side of a building. If water was pouring out onto gravel underneath, you'd find the largest pebbles directly under the spout. The lighter pebbles were picked up by the water current and carried away. As the current grows weaker, the larger rocks drop out of the stream. The lightest particles get carried the farthest away from the rain spout.

So, if you find that a green pen mark leaves a blue band of color with a yellow band above it, you now know at least two things: (1) the green pigment in the pen is actually made up of two colors, blue and yellow; and (2) the yellow color particles weigh less than the blue. Just like sand pebbles in a stream, the yellow was carried farther away, outside the blue.

Colors occur naturally in our most important organic sources (like the chemicals produced by plants and animals—especially plants). Scientists then use chromatography to separate and identify these substances by their color. From there, they can figure out how to make their own organic chemicals in the laboratory. Their chromatography is very sophisticated, but the results are no more colorful than your *own* Hidden Rainbows.

LAWN PAPER

LAWN PAPER

1/8 in = .32 cm	1/2 in = 1.27 cm
1/4 in = .64 cm	5 in = 12.7 cm
3 C = .72 l	8 in = 20.3 cm

The amount of time it takes to make Lawn Paper depends upon the drying method you choose. The paper itself can be prepared in about two hours.

YOU WILL NEED

Grass clippings
  (about one handful)
Scissors, measuring cup,
  paper towel
Blender or food processor
Water, newspaper
Piece of window screen
  (about 5″ × 8″)
Dishpan or tub or sink
Iron (optional)

Here's something to do with grass clippings that you probably never thought of: Make paper! Even though most of the world's paper is made from wood, many plant materials can be used: cotton, celery...even grass clippings. So grab a handful, and try it!

1 Use the scissors carefully to cut the grass into pieces about 1/4″ to 1/2″ long. You will need about one cup of chopped grass. Put the grass into the blender.

■ Cut a paper towel into 1/4″ pieces. Put the pieces in the blender with the grass.

PRESSING

LETTER

PICTURE FRAME

MOM DAD AND ME

DECORATIONS

CARDS

SHAPES

■ Add three cups of water to the paper and grass in the blender.

2 Blend the grass-paper-water mixture (called slurry) for three to five minutes or until it feels soft and smooth. Keep a close watch on your blender. If the grass is too long or there isn't enough water, your blender may have to work too hard and it will overheat. Add extra water so the grass doesn't get caught in the blades.

3 Pour off the excess water from the slurry and throw it away.
■ Put the screen into the dishpan or sink.
■ *Slowly* pour the slurry onto the screen in a thin, even layer. Use your hands to gently pat down, smooth any lumps, and fill in any holes. Flatten the slurry on the screen so it's smooth and flatter than a pancake.

4 Lay newspaper on top of the slurry. Pick a piece that doesn't have much dark print or else the wet lawn paper may absorb some of the dark ink.
■ With one hand under the screen and the other hand over the newspaper, carefully turn over the screen, slurry, and newspaper.

5 Press down hard on the screen to squeeze out water. Slowly peel up the screen so that your paper is left on the newspaper. If the paper sticks to the screen, keep pressing more water out of it.

■ Now keep pressing your lawn paper with dry newspaper. Press as hard as you can for a few minutes to flatten the grass and bind the fibers into paper.

6 To dry your paper, you can:
■ put it outside in a sunny spot.
■ put it in a solar greenhouse to dry it faster.
■ iron it dry in 10 minutes. Put the iron on the *cotton* setting. Protect your paper from heat by sandwiching it between layers of paper towels or newspaper.

7 When it is dry, carefully peel it away from the newspaper. Use your lawn paper for a special purpose:

■ Write a letter to a special person.
■ Take a picture of your family on the lawn or in your park. Frame the picture on a piece of lawn paper.
■ Have a lawn party with lawn-paper invitations and decorations.

VARIATIONS

■ Try making paper with dried grass instead of fresh, or cut up the leaves of a tree or shrub. How is this paper different from paper made from fresh grass?
■ Make colored paper by adding food coloring to the slurry. Or try using the newspaper comic pages in Step 4. They will also add color.
■ Be fancy. Press a dandelion or other pretty weed into the wet paper before pressing and drying.

■ Be creative. Shape the slurry on your screen into a shape, such as a dragon or a flower. Find things on your lawn to use as eyes and other details. Then press and dry it.

AFTERWORDS

Paper is a surprisingly recent invention. It was created less than 2,000 years ago by the Chinese. Conquering Arabs discovered this Chinese paper in 704 A.D., but it wasn't until about 600 years ago that paper came into common use in the West. In the Middle Ages, reading and learning were encouraged. This increased the demand for paper. As the demand increased through the centuries, the quality of paper was improved by experimenting with different raw materials.

Today, paper is made from cellulose pulp, which is found in all plant tissues and fibers. Fibers are thick-walled plant cells that support plant tissue. They are hollow tubes about ⅛" long and thinner than a hair. These tubes are reorganized to form thin sheets when paper is made. These thin, long cells give paper its toughness and flexibility.

Although any fiber may be used to make paper, certain fibers make higher quality paper than others. Linen is an excellent material for paper because its fibers have notches that help them stick to each other. Grass and straw have short, smooth fibers that cannot make strong papers alone. Adding other fibers, such as those in paper towels and newspaper, to grass fibers makes the lawn paper stronger. That is because paper towel and newspaper fibers are less smooth than grass fibers and help in binding the reorganized fibers into paper.

Today, about 95% of the world's paper is made from wood pulp, and there are about 12,000 types of paper manufactured. We use paper products every day. An average family discards one ton of paper each year—the amount of paper produced from 17 trees. That is a small forest every few years! Because of this, recycling centers have become valuable coordinators for the re-use of waste paper. Not only does recycling save trees, but it also uses 30% to 40% less energy than producing paper from new wood pulp. Try recycling a piece of your own lawn paper to prove this point.

Grass is almost everywhere—so why isn't grass made into paper? Grass is grown in wide-spread areas and the crop is bulky. Transportation costs alone make large-scale grass paper production more expensive than wood-pulp paper production. Also, the grass supply and its price vary from year to year. So grass paper production is held back by the difficulties of grass supply, rather than by any technical difficulties. These difficulties don't have to stop *you*. As long as you have a nearby lawn, park, or grassy traffic island, you can produce your own lawn paper.

BLEACH
BLUES

BLEACH BLUES

Tie-bleaching is a great way to give an old shirt a new look—and it's good *clean* fun! Do it on laundry day. It will take about an hour to tie-bleach one T-shirt.

YOU WILL NEED

Glass measuring cup
Liquid chlorine bleach
Newspapers
Cotton swabs, such as Q-Tips
Construction paper in various colors
Lemon juice
Old or new 100% cotton T-shirt in a color other than white
15 or 20 Rubber bands
Washing machine
Laundry detergent
A stick for stirring

Optional:
Blue jeans
White T-shirts and a box of dye

Have you ever seen tie-dyed T-shirts? This month, you can make some fabulous patterns by using tie-dye techniques *in reverse!* Just wrap some rubber bands around an old T-shirt, throw it in the washing machine, and let the chlorine bleach do the rest of the work. While you're at it, you may want to make yourself a pair of Bleach Blues. That's what we call blue jeans that have been bleached to show all their faded glory. Find out what else you can do with bleach—and get the laundry done at the same time—with this super-cool science activity!

1 Before you begin working with bleach: It's a good idea to change into old clothes, just in case you accidentally splash some bleach on yourself. Bleach should be handled very carefully. Avoid contact with your skin. Don't put your hands in the bleach and don't breathe the fumes.

Hold a glass measuring cup over a sink and carefully pour in a very small amount—a few tablespoons—of liquid chlorine bleach into the cup. Then go to a well-ventilated area or do this part of the activity outside. Spread out some old newspapers to work on. Dip the end of a cotton swab or Q-Tip into the bleach and use it to draw on a piece of colored construction paper. How quickly does the bleach work? Does it work just as fast on each color of paper?

Now try squirting a little lemon juice onto a piece of construction paper. Does it bleach the paper? (Be patient. It will take longer and the results will be less dramatic. But when the lemon juice is dry, you should see a light spot.)

**2 To tie-bleach one or more T-shirts, start by tying small sections of a 100% cotton T-shirt with rubberbands. Wrap the rubber bands *tightly* around each section of shirt—the tighter the better. If you want a large section to remain unbleached, then you will have to use lots of rubber bands there. *Hint:* Most rubber-band tying will make a circular pattern on your shirt. But if you want stripes, roll the shirt up like a jelly roll or sausage and then wrap the rubber bands around the sausage.

**3 Fill your washing machine one-fourth full with hot water. (On most washers, you can stop the machine from filling all the way by lifting the lid.) Pour in 3 or 4 cups of bleach—about 32 ounces. Add 1/4 cup of laundry detergent. Put your rubber-banded T-shirt into the washer and let it sit. (Don't close the lid because you don't want the washer to fill up any further yet!) Use a stick to stir the shirt around in the bleach. After 5 or 10 minutes, lift the shirt out with the stick and look at it. Has it faded some? If not, add more bleach to the water and let the shirt soak for another 10 minutes. Stir with the stick from time to time.

Note: When wet, your shirt won't look as faded or bleached as it probably is. Don't expect it to turn a pale, pale color. It will get lighter as it dries.

Leave the shirt in the bleach-water until it is noticeably lighter, then close the washing-machine lid and let it run through its cycle. That way the bleach will be completely rinsed from the T-shirt. Leave the rubber bands on until the shirt is completely washed and rinsed. Then take them off and either let the shirt dry on a hanger or throw it in the dryer.

HINTS FOR SUCCESS

■ Don't try to tie-bleach many different colored T-shirts together at the same time.

■ Tie the rubber bands very tightly, so that the bleach can't get to the tied parts of the shirt.

■ Use a lot of bleach. You may need to use as much bleach as water, so don't let the washing machine fill too much.

VARIATIONS

■ Try tie-bleaching a T-shirt using lemon juice—and the sun! Wrap the shirt with rubber bands, soak it in a sink partially filled with bottled lemon juice, and then put the shirt outside to dry in the sun for several hours. Don't remove the rubber bands until you think the sun has done its job.

■ If you want to make Bleach Blues—super-faded blue jeans—follow the instruc-

tions above beginning with Step 3. You can bleach blue jeans in the same washer load with your tie-bleach T-shirt *if* the T-shirt is also a dark color, like the jeans.

■ You can also tie-bleach shirts that have been dyed or tie-dyed first. Use 100% white cotton T-shirts and packaged dye. Follow the instructions on the package of dye. Make sure the dyed shirts are completely dry before you start to tie-bleach them. This is a good way to make several tie-bleached shirts to be given as gifts.

AFTERWORDS

Bleaching is a process that is performed on many products in this country, not just fabrics. Wheat, sugar, wood pulp and paper, furs, and human hair are all bleached using one of several different chemical compounds. These compounds, called *oxidizing agents,* include chlorine bleach, hydrogen peroxide, and sodium hypochlorite. All are acids, and basically they all work the same way: A chemical change takes place when the bleach reacts with oxygen. And any time a chemical change occurs in a substance, the chances are great—about 20 to 1—that the new substance will be white or colorless.

Can you see why lemon juice, an acid, might be able to bleach a cotton T-shirt if it's left out in the sun (exposed to oxygen) long enough? Actually, the sun does a very good job of bleaching fabrics, even without the help of lemon juice. You might find some examples of sun-bleaching in your house. Look at your couch or chair covers, and then find a place on the couch that *isn't* usually exposed to the sun. Furniture, wallpaper, photographs, books, papers, and even the clothing you wear are all affected by the sun's strong rays. It just takes the sun longer to bleach these things without the help of an oxdizing agent such as an acid.

Three hundred years ago, when linen and cotton fabrics were first bleached, the "acid" used was sour milk. The cloth was soaked for several weeks in sour milk, then washed and spread out on the grass for several more weeks, to bleach in the sun. Then that whole process was repeated five or six times! It took months to make cloth white.

Today, when fabric manufacturers bleach cotton industrially, the process not only whitens but also removes waxes, fats, and bits of brown husk that are present in the cotton plant. The cotton is bleached with hydrogen peroxide and other chemicals, and the cloth can be made white in a matter of *minutes!* Most cotton, linen, and silk fabrics are bleached *before* they are dyed.

The flour you eat in breads and cakes was actually bleached with some form of chlorine. You know that liquid chlorine laundry bleach is very harmful if swallowed. The secret to bleaching flour is that chlorine dioxide gas is used. In fact, the element chlorine itself is a gas. The slightly yellow or tan pigments in the flour are quickly bleached when they come into contact with the gas, but the flour itself absorbs very little chlorine.

What else gets bleached on a regular basis? Your hair does, if you swim in a chlorinated outdoor swimming pool. People often say that their hair gets sun-bleached in the summer sun, but they're only half right. It's usually the combination of chlorine from a pool and the exposure to the air that does the best "bleach job."

Wood pulp too is chemically bleached so that plain white paper can be made from trees that were obviously not white to start with. Even for wood pulp that is only going to be made into something brown—like a cardboard carton—some bleaching is required. In that case, the bleach doesn't necessarily make the pulp white, but it does remove the part of the pulp that isn't useful in paper-making.

FOR MORE INFORMATION . . .

Places to Write and Visit

Here are some places you can write or visit for more information about color and light. When you write, include your name and address, and be specific about the information you would like to receive. Don't forget to enclose a stamped, self-addressed envelope for a reply.

American Museum of Science and Energy
300 S. Tulane Avenue
Oak Ridge, TN 37830

Edison Electric Institute
1111 19th Street, N.W.
Washington, D.C. 20036

Maryland Science Center
601 Light Street
Baltimore, MD 21230

Discovery World Museum of Science, Economics,
    and Technology
818 W. Wisconsin Avenue
Milwaukee, WI 53233

The MIT Museum
265 Massachusetts Avenue
Cambridge, MA 02139

Further Reading about Color and Light

Here are more books you can read about color and light. Check your local library or bookstore to see if they have the books or can order them for you.

Connecting Rainbows. Stanish (Good Apple)
I Can Make a Rainbow. Frank (Incentive Publications)
Light and Color. Anderson (Raintree)
Light and Lasers. Whyman (Watts)
Light Fantastic. Watson (Lothrop)
Looking at Light and Color. Hill and Hill (Trafalgar Square)
The Science Book of Color. Ardley (Harcourt Brace)
The Science Book of Light. Ardley (Harcourt Brace)

Hands-On Facts about Color and Light

Did you know . . .

- the "Evening Star" isn't really a star at all? It's the planet Venus.

- the sky isn't really blue, or any other color, for that matter? It often looks blue because of gases, dust, and vapors in the air that scatter and reflect light from the sun. Blue light is most easily scattered, so the sky most often looks blue.

- an average family throws away an amount of paper in one year that is equivalent to 17 trees? Obviously, this paper should be recycled, or soon there will be no more trees — and no more paper!

- you can tell planets from stars in the night sky? — Planets don't "twinkle."

- the color of an object is really the result of whichever color from the light spectrum the object reflects? The colors from the spectrum you don't see are absorbed by the object.

- size really can make a difference in the animal world? Animals with big ears are likely to hear better than those with small ears; large eyes allow more light to enter the eye and thus make an animal's eyesight more acute.

- strobe lights are not just used in discos to create flashy effects, but are also used for testing purposes in industry and technology?

- neither the sun nor the moon nor the stars actually "rise" or "set?" They only appear to because of the rotation of the Earth.

- there are more than 12,000 types of paper manufactured in the world today?

- the first cameras were entire rooms completely sealed off from light, except for one small hole through which an image appeared projected on the opposite wall?

GLOSSARY

acid: a chemical compound with a sour taste. Acids turn blue litmus paper red when diluted in water.

Alpha Centauri: the star that is closest to Earth, after the sun.

base: a chemical substance that tastes bitter. Bases turn red litmus paper blue.

camera obscura: a Latin term meaning "dark chamber." The camera obscura was originally a darkened room with a hole in one wall. The image of whatever was in the room on the other side of the hole was projected onto the wall opposite the hole.

cellulose pulp: a substance found in all plant tissues and fibers that is used in making paper.

chromatography: a branch of science that identifies different substances by their color reactions.

coherent light: the concentrated light produced by a laser beam.

cones: cells in the eye that are sensitive to color.

galaxy: A very large grouping of celestial bodies. Our solar system is just a part of one such vast galaxy called the Milky Way.

hard water: water with a high mineral content.

infrared light: light with a wavelength that is just beyond the red end of the visible spectrum.

laser: a beam of light in which all waves are exactly the same length and moving together as one.

nocturnal: preferring to be active at night, rather than during the day.

oxidizing agent: a compound such as chlorine bleach or hydrogen peroxide that causes a chemical change in a substance that leaves it colorless.

photosynthesis: the process by which plants convert sunlight into nutrients. Photosynthesis begins when chlorophyll in the leaves is activated by sunlight.

pigment: a substance that gives color; plants and animals carry pigments in their tissue that cause their fur or skin to be characteristic colors.

prism: a piece of glass that disperses white light into the full spectrum of colors.

recycling: re-using something, or collecting it to be re-processed so that it can then be used again.

retina: a lining on the inside of the eye, containing the rods and cones that are sensitive to light and color.

rods: cells in the eye that are sensitive to light.

spectrum: the visible spectrum of colors that make up white light: red, orange, yellow, green, blue, and violet.

strobe light: a light that pulsates on and off in a regular rhythm.

INDEX